IMAGES
of America

HIGHLAND AND
THE TOWN OF LLOYD

A temporary gateway set up next to the Methodist church on Vineyard Avenue proclaims "Highland the Gateway to Ulster County." The date is August 24, 1915, and the whole town is decked out for a celebration that was called "Glad Day," which marked the opening of a new state road to Highland from the riverfront. The pictures on page 117 show why everyone was glad to have the new road. (Courtesy of Gail Russell.)

On the cover: In 1897, trolley tracks were laid from the riverfront through Highland and all the way to New Paltz. Main Street remained a dirt road until 1903, when this picture was taken, showing the installation of a brick pavement. The left corner, where the First National Bank of Highland erected a stately limestone bank building in 1923, was occupied by Deyo's Hall, which had storefronts at street level and meeting rooms above the stores. (Courtesy of the Lloyd Town Historian's Office.)

IMAGES
of America

HIGHLAND AND THE TOWN OF LLOYD

Ethan P. Jackman

ARCADIA
PUBLISHING

Published by Arcadia Publishing
Charleston, South Carolina

Library of Congress Control Number: 2008938752

For all general information contact Arcadia Publishing at:
Telephone 843-853-2070
Fax 843-853-0044
E-mail sales@arcadiapublishing.com
For customer service and orders:
Toll-Free 1-888-313-2665

Visit us on the Internet at www.arcadiapublishing.com

CONTENTS

ACKNOWLEDGMENTS

In 2008, the author was appointed as Lloyd town historian by supervisor Raymond J. Costantino, who encouraged the publication of this book, and the town's archives and facilities made it possible. Most of the illustrations in this book had been collected many years ago and were in the town's historical archive. We must thank the previous town historians who collected them, and the citizens who donated them to the town. In most cases, we do not know from what source a particular picture originated, but the names of certain town historians appear over and over again in the archives.

Many of the earliest pictures have Mabel Lent's name on their backs. Beatrice Wadlin's name appears on a large number of pictures, and many pictures were found with notes written by Dottie Gruner. Of those three former town historians, only Dottie Gruner is still with us, and it has been a pleasure to discuss historical questions with her on numerous occasions. In this book, unless another acknowledgment appears with an image, the picture was obtained from the town's archive, including ones donated by the author.

Other pictures have been contributed by private collectors, notably Vivian Yess Wadlin and Gail Russell. Town clerk Rosaria Schiavone Peplow and the rest of the town hall staff were sources of both pictures and a wealth of information. Sal Timperio was very kind to let us borrow several of the pictures that adorn the walls of his restaurant.

Many of the pictures were recently printed from a cache of early-20th-century glass-plate negatives, and they are being published for the first time in this book. We are not certain of whom the photographer was, but some of the plates were donated while Dottie Gruner was town historian, and others that appear to be by the same photographer were recently donated to the town's archive by Tim Harnett, who had bought the plates at a yard sale.

INTRODUCTION

The present-day town of Lloyd was originally the eastern part of New Paltz Township. The Huguenot founders of New Paltz were quite content with their settlement on the Wallkill River, and at first they paid little attention to the eastern part of their domain.

The first settlement in present-day Lloyd was near the Hudson River. In 1754, Anthony Yelverton, the son of a Poughkeepsie magistrate of the same name, came across the river with equipment to start a sawmill. He built a house for himself partly with the timbers from an old boat, and today that house is the oldest wooden building still standing on its original site in Ulster County. It is listed on the National Register of Historic Places.

Yelverton also needed bricks for the fireplaces in his house, so he started a brickyard to make them. When more settlers arrived, he opened Lloyd's first store in the lower level of his house. He also started the first ferry service to Poughkeepsie, using flat boats rowed by slaves.

The settlement at the river was at first called Yelverton's Landing. After Valentine Baker built an inn at the landing in 1785, the area was called Baker's Landing for awhile, later New Paltz Landing, and finally Highland Landing.

During the War for Independence there were no battles fought in the area, but in the fall of 1777, British general John Vaughan sailed up the Hudson River with a large fleet and 1,600 troops that were headed for Saratoga to join Gen. John Burgoyne. All along their route, the British shot hot cannon balls to set fire to colonists' property, but they missed Yelverton's holdings. When excavations were made for a new sewer plant opposite the Yelverton house, British cannonballs were unearthed. Vaughan reached Kingston on October 16, 1777, and burned the city. But he was too late to accomplish his real mission; by the time his troops reached Saratoga, General Burgoyne had already surrendered.

Although Yelverton came through the British foray unscathed, he suffered a great loss some years later. Legend has it that while crossing the river on his ferry, the boat capsized. Yelverton was able to swim to the shore, but about a dozen of his slaves drowned. It is believed that the slaves are buried on the hill behind the house. Yelverton continued to operate the ferry service until his death in 1792, and Noah Elting then began to operate a ferry service to Poughkeepsie.

An observer in 1795 described the ferryboat as "a large raft-like boat with a sail and large sweeps [oars] for sculling [rowing]." It could carry a few wagons and passengers. Some later ferries on the Hudson River were powered by horses on treadmills, until steam power took over after 1820. During most of the 19th century, steamboats carried freight and passengers from the riverfront landing to New York City.

There are no incorporated villages in the town of Lloyd, but the largest community is Highland. While the earliest settlement in Lloyd was at the riverfront, inland from the river other settlers were starting farms in the late 1700s. Around 1820, one of the farmers, Philip Elting, who owned much of the land where the Highland business district is today, decided to start his own village. He built several stores and donated land for the first Methodist church building where the route between Newburgh and Kingston intersected with the road to the river. Skeptics ridiculed Elting's enterprise as "Philip's Folly" and "Cow Town," but gradually the new village began to grow.

As early as 1833, settlers in the eastern part of the township circulated petitions to secede from New Paltz, and the state legislature established the Town of Lloyd in 1845. There are several theories about why the name Lloyd was chosen, but the origin of that name is shrouded in mystery. What is known is that the original spelling was Loyd, and a post office named Loyd opened five miles west of the river in 1844. The records of the legislative proceedings in the 1840s referred to the proposed town as Loyd, but when the act establishing the new town was finally passed and published, the name was spelled Lloyd, so that is the official spelling.

The first post office in the town was established in 1821 and named New Paltz Landing. It was located in a now-forgotten village called Nippityville, north of Elting's new village, at the junction of North Road and Grand Street. Even after the separation of Lloyd from New Paltz Township in 1845, mail coming to the eastern part of Lloyd had to be addressed to New Paltz Landing and often wound up in the village of New Paltz by mistake. In 1865, a meeting was held to address that issue and the fact that Elting's village never had an official name. Although there are different opinions about who suggested the name of Highland, that was the name which was chosen, probably because the village was on the highland above the river.

As time progressed, many businesses at the riverfront relocated to Philip Elting's new village, especially after several fires destroyed much of the commercial area at the river. But Highland was not immune to fires, and on March 17, 1891, the west side of the Vineyard Avenue business district was wiped out by a blaze that consumed eight of the principal structures. Fire struck again on the same site in 1948 and again in 1979. The latest building at that location, built as a memorial to Highland contractor Eugene Ossie, is constructed of steel and concrete so as to be fireproof.

Highland became a focal point of railroad activity in the latter part of the 19th century, when railroads surpassed steamboats as the most efficient mode of transportation between Albany and New York City. The Highland station on the West Shore Railroad continued in service through the 1930s. The Central New England Railway brought passengers and freight to Highland over the colossal Poughkeepsie–Highland Railroad Bridge. An electric railroad, or trolley line, was completed in 1897, and it took railway and ferry passengers from the riverfront westward to a growing number of summer resorts. The Highland trolley also had a connection to the railroad bridge in its early years, and a small steam locomotive, called the "Dinky," would link up with the trolley cars to take passengers over the river to Poughkeepsie.

In trying to tell the history of a town with pictures, we are limited by the photographic material that is available. We regret that many significant developments and places had to be omitted because no suitable pictures could be found or those pictures that were available did not meet the standards for publication.

In this book, the street names, place names, and house numbers referred to are those as they exist in 2009.

One

THE HIGHLAND
BUSINESS DISTRICT

This journey into the past begins with some of the earliest photographs of "downtown" Highland. These pictures, which were taken from stereoscopic view cards, show what the village looked like before a disastrous fire struck on the night of March 17, 1891. The largest store in town was the general store of William E. Wilcox. It was also the first store to be rebuilt after the fire, and accounts said that Wilcox had a temporary store erected while some of the ashes were still smoldering.

Highland learned its lesson from the fire of 1891—namely that more than the old bucket brigade was needed to fight fires. The Highland Water Company was formed the following year, and it proceeded to construct a reservoir on Illinois Mountain and to install water lines to serve the village. When that was completed and an abundant supply of water was available, a fire company, Highland Hose Company No. 1, was incorporated in 1895.

Many merchants replaced their establishments with brick buildings, several of which are as useful today as when they were first constructed. The new brick Wilcox store was the centerpiece of Highland for 56 years, but it was destroyed by another fire in 1948. Today the Ossie Building stands on the Wilcox site.

This is how Highland looked before the fire of 1891. As the village is approached from the river (left), first is the Tillson Building, which was occupied by various tenants. That was where the fire started, and the cause was never ascertained. The three-story Miller Building next to it housed Carpenter's law office, the Highland Cornet Band, and several other tenants. At the intersection of Vineyard Avenue and Main Street (below), the W. E. Wilcox dry goods store can be seen on the left. The large building on the right is Deyo's Hall, later called the DeGraff building, where the bank building stands today.

Here is another view looking north on Vineyard Avenue. The Wilcox store employs a unique advertising device, a wagon and a farmer on its porch roof. The next building is George Rose's store and then the Miller and Tillson buildings, which each housed several tenants—businesses on the lower floors and apartments above them.

Behind the stores on Vineyard Avenue, the Blue Mills were powered by the flow of the Twaalfskill Creek. This is the entrance to it from Milton Avenue. Shown in this c. 1880 stereoscopic view, the mill was first operated by William Henry Deyo. Still operating in the 1920s, it was later known as Traphagen's mill. (Courtesy of Vivian Yess Wadlin.)

HIGHLAND

C.A.B. Love

H. Trapagan

Baptist Ch.
H. Ostrander
J. Wiley
A.T.

Taylor

KINGSTON ROAD

O.H. Elting

C. Elting

C.W. Elting

NEW PALTZ TURNPIKE

O.H. Elting

Mrs. C. Woolsey

N. Carpenter

J.H. Brinkerhoff

C. Perkins
C.J. Deyo
P. Schwab
C. Harr

Parsonage

Felly Fact.

Post Office
B. Dobbs

PRES. CH.

J. Breed

Heston
Mrs.
Galloway
B.H. Bevier

J.P.

A.P.

CHURCH ST.

SEMINARY

J.J.H.

J.J.H.

Mrs. Deyo

S.D. Bond Hotel

Dr. Hull

M.E. Ch.

Dr.
G. Vor.
Ward
G. Vor.

R.
Dubois

L.B.D. Deyo
J.
Perkins
S. Vor.

C.
Vie

B.

DEYO

Deyo House

S. Ranson

MAIN ST.

E.A. Deyo

I.D. Bond

Wildow
J.C. Dubois

L.J. Hasbrouck
S. Saxton

J.R. Wisemiller

S.D. Bond

J. Elmendough

WHITE ST.

VINEYARD AVE

J.R. Hasbrouck

P. LeFever · D. L. Bernard

R. F. Allen

L. Miller

SCHOOL · M. Parrott

C. D.

F. Jones · LANE

A. Maltby · C. D. · J. W. Thorn

C. Seymour

C. Devoe

H. pheer · P. V. Mitchell's SEMINARY & Res. & Grounds

GRAND · Spencer · Adams

W. SASH · ington

EPIS. Ch. · WILCOX · G. Willsie · Turner

LLOYD · HO. · AVE. · J. Worden

Store · J. V. Freer · Mrs. C. Piper

Toll Gate · BRIDGE ST. AVE.

R. D. Perkins · C. Perkins

G. Haight

W. Deyo Sash & Blind Fact.

H. Ormsby · MILL

A. Brinckerhoff

In 1875, the F. W. Beers Company published an atlas of all of the towns in Ulster County, complete with the buildings that were standing at that time and the names of their owners. Although the layout of the streets has not changed very much, some of their names were different. The name of Vineyard Avenue was used for the part of the street that started at Church Street, while what is now called Vineyard Avenue was then named Main Street. What is now called Main Street was then the New Paltz Turnpike. In the upper left, the Kingston Road is now North Road. In this book, all references to street names use the names as they are known in 2009.

13

This building, which still stands on the corner of Grand Street and River Road, is the oldest store building still standing in Highland. Built in 1831 as Richard Woolsey's store, it was R. D. Perkins's store in the 1880s. It was also the Lloyd Hotel for a period, before being converted to its present use as apartments. (Courtesy of Vivian Yess Wadlin.)

This picture, taken about 1887, shows the Highland Cornet Band in front of its band room in the Miller building. Seen here are, from left to right, (first row) Albert Rose and DuBois Hasbrouck (alto), John O'Bryn (snare drum), Hubert Elting (baritone), Charlie Freer and an unidentified Newburg man (trombone), and Dan Brauvelt (bass); (second row) William Eckert (cymbals), Duane Eckert (band leader and cornet), Charles Terwilliger (bass drum), Heston Simpson and I. Collins (cornet), Ed Kipp (tenor?), and an unidentified Newburg man (cornet or clarinet).

This is what Highland's business district looked like on March 18, 1891. Eight of the principal commercial buildings on the east side of Vineyard Avenue were been completely destroyed during the previous night, and all that is left are their stone foundations. In the upper right is the roof of Deyo's Hall, on the other side of the street, which was not damaged by the fire.

An astonished crowd gathers outside of the Methodist Church on Vineyard Avenue to view the remains of Highland's business district, while others are seen walking among the stone foundations, which are all that is left of the village's principal commercial buildings. To the right is the Methodist parsonage behind the church.

No sooner was the fire out then Highland was being rebuilt. William E. Wilcox is setting up a temporary store (right), and the horse-drawn vehicle, called an express wagon, is bringing supplies. In the wagon are some of the businessmen who lost their buildings. One is identified as being either Samuel Miller of the Miller building or hardware dealer Charles Feeter.

Here are the men of Highland Hose Company No. 1, around 1900, together with their hand-drawn hose cart, ladder, axes, and horns. This all-volunteer company consisted of many of the leading Highland businessmen, whose property the firemen stood ready to protect. On bended knee in the front row with horns are (from left to right) Byron Clearwater, Orange Ingraham, and John J. Clearwater.

Here is the new downtown Highland with brick buildings erected in 1891. On the left is the new Rose building, which housed J. W. Feeter's hardware store and Rose's Hall on the second floor. To the right of the Rose building is the new Wilcox building. Actually consisting of three storefronts, W. E. Wilcox had a harness shop on the left side, a dry goods store in the middle, a grocery on the right, and meeting rooms upstairs. (Courtesy of Sal Timperio.)

Here is an inside view of the new 1891 Wilcox dry goods store, looking in from the Vineyard Avenue entrance toward the rear of the building. Note the modern gas lighting fixtures and fashionable wainscoted ceiling. The plain tables displaying domestics on the left would soon be replaced by more stylish counters, similar to those on the right.

Looking down Vineyard Avenue from the south, the first building has the office of the *Highland Post* on its right side and a drugstore on the left. In between them is the entrance to the upper stories. Then comes the Wilcox building. The next building was a hardware store from 1891 until it became Vadala's Pharmacy in the 1990s. The next building is also still standing, and since 1969, it has been occupied by Three Guys Pizza. (Courtesy of Sal Timperio.)

This is Upright's new hotel, and it opened around 1895. It was built on the site of their first hotel, which was destroyed in the fire of 1891, at 54 Vineyard Avenue today. Martin Upright was a member of the first fire company, and the Upright family was active in civic affairs through the 1950s. This image is from a glass-plate negative. (Courtesy of Tim Harnett.)

The north side of Main Street is seen in this *c.* 1900 picture. The one-story building in the foreground is Maynard's Meat Market. Byron Clearwater's store is the two-story building next to Maynard's. Note the trolley car coming down the street at the far left. At the top left in the distance is the new Elting house, built in 1897, now the Michael Torsone Memorial Funeral Home.

Highland's citizens have turned out to honor their firemen in this *c.* 1900 parade up Vineyard Avenue. Firemen's parades have long been a tradition in Ulster County, with Highland Hose Company No. 1 both hosting them and participating in the parades held in other towns. This image is from a glass-plate negative. (Courtesy of Tim Harnett.)

When this picture was taken in December 1914, the gaslights in the Wilcox store had already been replaced by electric lights. The wiring for them is the "knob and tube" system originated by Thomas A. Edison. Note the sets of two electric wires running along the surface of the ceiling, and switches hanging down to be within reach.

J. W. FEETER,

HIGHLAND, N. Y.

HARDWARE, PLUMBING, SLATING.

STOVES AND RANGES.

HEATING A SPECIALTY.

Sporting Goods, Bicycles, Kodak Supplies, Phonographs and Sundries.

This is an advertising card for J. W. Feeter's hardware store. This particular card, together with other artifacts, was found inside the cornerstone of the 1903 Highland School building when the building was demolished. Feeter's store was located on Vineyard Avenue next to and south of the Wilcox building.

This was a scene in front of the Kenilworth building, which dominated the northeast corner of Vineyard and Milton Avenues with a circular tower. Around 1900, it housed Erichsen's Meat Market, which wanted to let customers know about its freshly butchered venison.

This whimsical postcard from around 1900 depicts Highland "in the near future," bustling with trolleys and automobiles going in every direction and even an aerial tramway. Business really was booming around this time, with two railroads, a trolley line, and ferries all bringing commerce through Highland. (Courtesy of Gail Russell.)

Highland has always paid special honor to its veterans. These Civil War veterans pose outside of Highland's Methodist church around 1900 for a reunion of the Grand Army of the Republic. A monument to the 156th Regiment of Civil War volunteers was erected in 1908 and still stands at the entrance to Highland.

On August 29, 1919, Highland citizens are waiting to welcome the soldiers who are returning from the Great War (later named World War I). On the left side of Vineyard Avenue, Smith's Garage can be seen, and on the right is Whittley's tailor shop. (Courtesy of Gail Russell.)

All of the buildings in Highland are draped with flags on World War I Welcome Day, as the crowd anxiously awaits the arrival of the troops by train at Highland Landing (above). The Wilcox building (with the arch on top) was often the backdrop for civic events in the center of town. Having defeated "Kaiser Bill and the Huns of Germany," the proud soldiers march for the last time up Vineyard Avenue (below). One of the town's most legendary characters, Levi Calhoun, served in the army for one week before being discharged, but when the troops came home, he put on his uniform and joined in the parade.

Here are some more scenes of the tremendous Welcome Day celebration for the returning veterans of World War I on August 29, 1919. Sailors are also welcomed home with a ride in this early pickup truck (above). The square in front of the Methodist church (below) was where welcoming speeches were given. Since that time, this has been the traditional place for ceremonies honoring veterans from the town of Lloyd on Memorial Day and Veterans Day of each year.

This picture shows the World War I troops being mustered out in front of Smith's Garage, which was located at 79 Vineyard Avenue. Across the street is the Great Atlantic and Pacific Tea Company's grocery store, later abbreviated as the A&P.

In 1926, a memorial was dedicated to the soldiers who served during World War I. It consists of a flagpole with a base that has the names of all of the veterans on it. It was donated by Rep. Harcourt J. Pratt, the son of Highland businessman George W. Pratt.

The Park Filling Station on the southeast corner of Vineyard and Milton Avenues was a good place for a fill-up in the 1930s. Operated by Livingston Rhodes, son of Civil War veteran Aaron Rhodes, it also sold snacks such as hot dogs and Highland brand ice cream.

The Highland Drum Corps parades down Main Street around 1935. On the left corner is the First National Bank of Highland and on the right is Maynard's Meat Market. Note the four-sided illuminated sign in the center of the street, which advised motorists "Slow Keep Right."

Harry Maynard and his staff pose outside Maynard's Market in 1909. The original building is still standing at 1 Main Street, with a second story that was added about 1920 (see page 29). For many years, this has been the home of the Little Flower Shop.

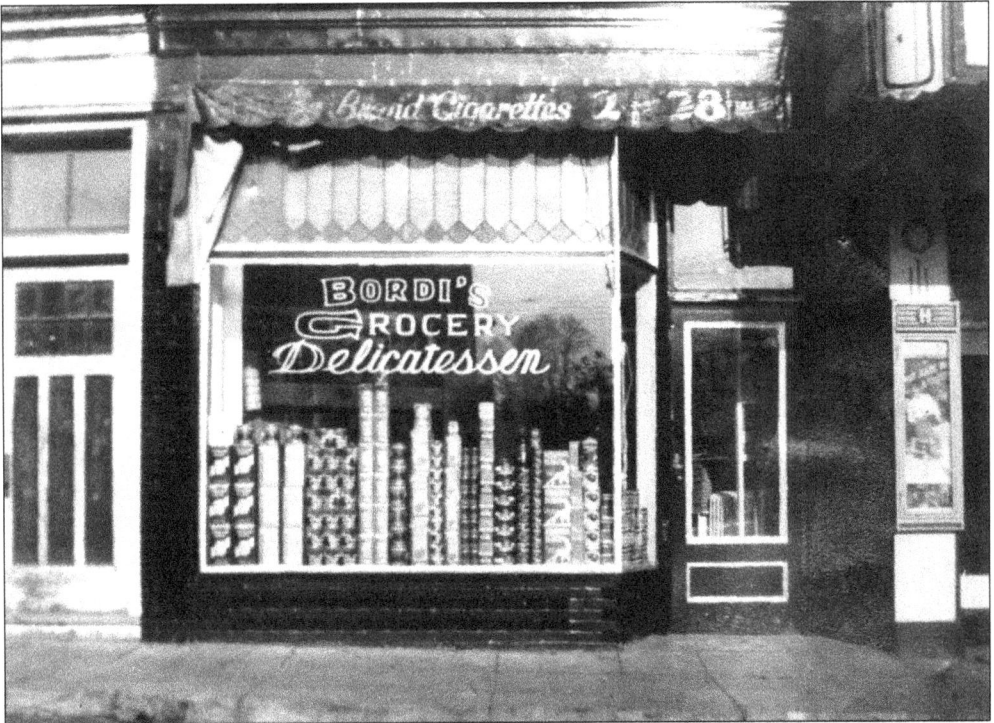

Another familiar store on Vineyard Avenue in the 1930s was Bordi's Grocery and Delicatessen, located in the since-demolished Highland Movie Theater building at 95 Vineyard Avenue. Originally operated by John Bordi Sr., this store relocated a few doors north and continued in business through the 1990s. (Courtesy of Sal Timperio.)

This building, at 24 Main Street, housed the Lent Law Office. It is on the site of a house built in 1814 by Noah Elting. On August 25, 1930, it was decorated to welcome Gov. Franklin D. Roosevelt to Highland for the opening of the Mid-Hudson Bridge. The unusual staircase in front was originally a platform at the right height to step into and out of carriages. Inside the Lent Law Office (below) are, from left to right, Harold Lent, Mrs. Everett (secretary), Abram Lent, and Andrew W. Lent.

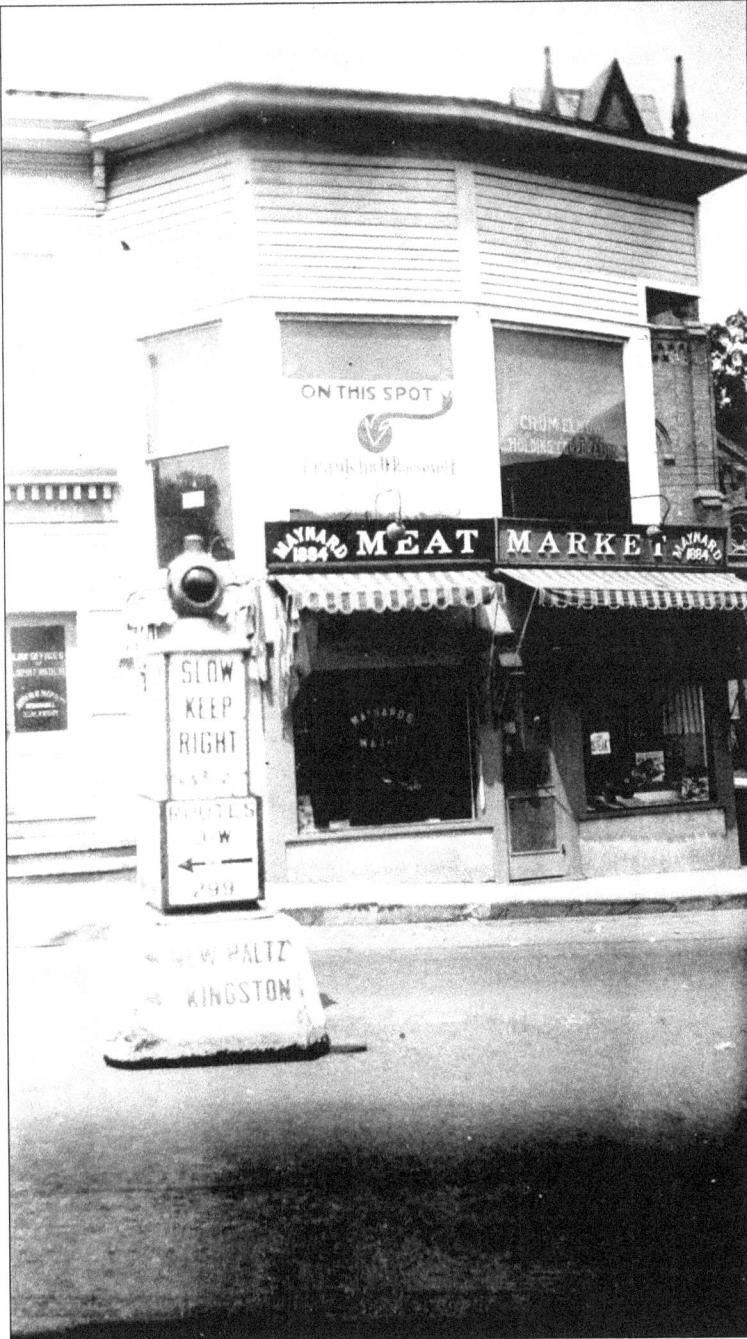

Not everyone in Highland welcomed Roosevelt. Although he was elected as president four times, he never once carried the town of Lloyd or his native town of Hyde Park in Dutchess County. Visible in the window above Maynard's Meat Market is a large sign that reads "On this spot Franklin D. Roosevelt told 3 lies." In the 1930s, the editor of the weekly *Highland Post* newspaper regularly ran editorials castigating President Roosevelt. They were so strong that Roosevelt decided to reply to them, and the local newspaper suddenly received national attention. (Courtesy of Vivian Yess Wadlin.)

One could buy anything that a household might need on Vineyard Avenue in the 1930s and souvenirs of Highland too (note the sign hanging below the "drugs" sign). Posing in front of the A&P market are, from left to right, Mike Milano, unidentified, Sam A. Castellano, and unidentified. Some of these men worked in the store's butcher shop.

This scene shows Vineyard Avenue around 1935, with no less than three drugstores. Vadala's Cut-Rate Drugs remained in the building on the left until the 1990s, when it moved to the former hardware store at 62 Vineyard Avenue. On the far right is the Kenilworth Building at 86 Vineyard Avenue, now the home of Brennie's Pizzeria. (Courtesy of Sal Timperio.)

Here Main Street is seen on a winter day about 1935, looking west from near the bank building (above). On the right side of the street, the grill and barbershop (with pole mounted outside) are in a building that was located at 21 Main Street. On the left side of the street is the Lent Law Office at 24 Main Street. On the top of the hill is a home built by the Elting family in 1897, now the Michael Torsone Memorial Funeral Home. Looking east from the corner of Church Street (below), these buildings are seen from a different perspective, and the Wilcox building is straight ahead on Vineyard Avenue. (Courtesy of Vivian Yess Wadlin.)

These images look inside some Highland stores in the 1930s. In the hardware store (above), J. J. Ennist (on the right in the rear of the store) has bought out J. W. Feeter, and he includes washing machines and lawn mowers among his wares. The man on the left is Harvey Traver, and the man in the middle wearing the stylish straw hat is probably a customer. Electrician Walter A. Seaman has opened a lighting showroom (below). He would later buy out Ennist's hardware business. (Courtesy of Gail Russell.)

This Highland grocery store (above) was owned by Lorin Callahan (left), who later was elected as Lloyd town clerk. In a 1931 picture of the Wilcox store (below), the primitive electric wiring on the ceiling has been replaced, and there appears to be much less stock than what the store carried in its heyday. The saleswoman on the right is Caroline Atkins, and the one on the left is unidentified. Wilcox's grocery department, which was in the right storefront of his building, has since been leased to the Grand Union Company. (Above, courtesy of Lloyd town clerk Rosaria Schiavone Peplow.)

The town of Lloyd's World War II Honor Roll (above) listed all of the veterans from the town who served from 1941 to 1945. It was located in a vacant lot on Vineyard Avenue between Smith's Garage (left) and the First National Bank. In 1952, the bank built an addition on this lot. The names of the veterans of World War II are inscribed in a bronze book that was placed in the wall of the town hall meeting room. The town of Lloyd, the American Legion, and the Veterans of Foreign Wars have never failed to honor the town's veterans each Memorial Day. The scene below, from around 1950, shows a ceremony at the World War I memorial flagpole in front of the Methodist church.

The end of the Wilcox store came on January 28, 1948. A fire broke out next door in Walter Seaman's (formerly J. J. Ennist's) hardware store, which sustained moderate damage. The blaze quickly spread to the Wilcox building, which was destroyed. Wilcox never reopened his business, but the Grand Union Superette in the right side of the building did relocate in the village.

This is how the downtown area looked in the 1960s, with a modern two-story building taking the place of the Wilcox store. It housed various businesses, including Harry Fogle's drugstore and the Savings and Loan Association of Kingston. This structure was destroyed by fire in 1979, and the site remained vacant until 1988, when construction of the Ossie Building was started.

Since 1942, the Highland Post Office had been located in the former Smith's Garage building, after the automobile dealership moved to Route 9W. A larger post office was needed, and the town of Lloyd also wanted a new town hall. These two functions were combined in the new building shown in this 1952 postcard.

The new building was dedicated by Eleanor Roosevelt on November 22, 1952. The town built the one-story structure, but only needed half of one floor for its offices, so it leased the other half to the post office. The post office moved out in 1972, and the town government has grown so much that it not only needed the whole first floor, but a second story had to be added on top of that.

Lloyd town officials for 1952 are shown above in the town hall meeting room. From left to right are Frank Marx (water and sewer departments), William Upright (councilman, and later town justice), Albert Lester (councilman), Harry Collier (councilman), John Gaffney (supervisor), Herman Sandy (councilman), Allen F. Decker Sr. (highway superintendent), J. J. Ennist (town justice), and Lorin Callahan (town clerk). In the picture below, town clerk Lorin S. Callahan is serving a citizen in his new town hall office. When Callahan retired in 1959, he had served as town clerk for 46 years, the longest continuous term of any town clerk in the State of New York. (Courtesy of Lloyd town clerk Rosaria Schiavone Peplow.)

Highland's volunteer fire department shows off its equipment around 1960. Seen behind this new garage on the corner of Main and Church Streets is the roof of the 1922 firehouse, with a siren on top of it. On the north side of Main Street is the Sugar Bowl Restaurant, which was operated for many years by Danny and Marge Canora. (Courtesy of the Southern Ulster County Chamber of Commerce.)

Now standing on the site where three previous fires destroyed buildings in downtown Highland is the Ossie Building, built as a memorial to Highland contractor Eugene Ossie. Construction started around 1988, but stopped abruptly, leaving just the shell of the building standing. The interior was completed in 2001 by Ethan P. Jackman.

Two

HIGHLAND INSTITUTIONS
AND LANDMARKS

As Highland developed into the largest community in the town of Lloyd, it also became the center of civic life. Churches of several denominations, public and private schools, fraternal societies, as well as scores of businesses, all were established in Highland during the 19th and 20th centuries. When the First National Bank of Highland opened for business in 1900, the future looked bright, and nobody was joking about "Philip's Folly" anymore.

Fraternal orders and civic organizations flourished in the days before electronic forms of entertainment. Many of the store buildings in the business district were built with halls on their second stories, which were rented to organizations and for social and business functions. The Town of Lloyd often rented space on the second floor of the Wilcox building to hold meetings and elections. Part of that floor housed the Masonic Temple.

Next to the Wilcox building, Rose's Hall occupied the upper floor of the store at 62 Vineyard Avenue. Across the street, Deyo's Hall on the southwest corner of Vineyard Avenue and Main Street (now the bank corner) had its second-floor space leased to the Sunshine Lodge of the International Order of Odd Fellows (IOOF). The local Lion's Club was organized in 1930.

The above organizations were for men only, but the ladies had their own exclusive all-women organizations. The Women's Christian Temperance Union, a national organization whose purpose was to promote abstinence from alcoholic drinks, had an active Highland chapter from the 1890s through the 1940s. The Music Study Club gave performances at Lakeledge, the Tillson estate south of the village. But no organization was more exclusive than the U.D.s, a club of 25 ladies whose name was so secret that only two members were allowed to know what *U.D.* stood for.

A Presbyterian congregation was formed in 1792, and in 1797, its church was erected on Route 44/55 at the corner of Chapel Hill Road, near the Presbyterian cemetery. The present Highland Presbyterian Church on Church Street was a small building when it was constructed in 1844, and it was nicknamed the "White Church." The building was enlarged and the fine Greek Revival portico was added in 1871. The house to the right of the church was built in 1912 as the Presbyterian manse (pastor's residence). An addition with new Sunday school rooms was constructed in 1954. (Left, courtesy of Vivian Yess Wadlin.)

The Methodist Episcopal Church, now the United Methodist Church, established its first building on the site of the present brick church in 1821. Highland founder Philip Elting donated the land. When the present edifice was erected in 1869, the original building was moved to a lot on Main Street, where it continued to be used for offices until its demolition in the 1960s. The picture at right shows the building in about 1900 with its original spires, which have since been removed. When it was built, provision was made to install a clock in the tower, but the clock was not installed until 1906. The picture below shows the east side of the church and the rectory behind it in about 1900.

A Roman Catholic mission was established in the town of Lloyd in 1899 by St. James Church in Milton, and St. Augustine's Church was erected in 1900. This picture shows the original wood frame building. The Highland church continued to be a mission of the Milton church until 1950, when Highland became a separate parish. Also in 1950, the house to the left of the church was purchased to serve as a rectory, and a redbrick facade was installed on both the rectory and the church. Parochial school classes were held in the basement of the church until 1959, when St. Augustine's Parochial School opened on the corner of Philips Avenue and Elting Place. (Courtesy of Sal Timperio.)

The picture above shows parishioners dressed for mass at the new St. Augustine's Church on a cold winter day around 1905. The c. 1950 postcard below shows the brick front and also the rectory. The peaked front windows and doors of the church were squared off in the 1950 remodeling, and the main entrance was relocated to the middle of the front. The original structure remains behind the brick facade.

Catholic Church, Highland, N. Y.

Highland's smallest church building is the Episcopal Church of the Holy Trinity on Grand Street, which opened in 1873. The stone used in building the structure was donated by Oliver J. Tillson, and the land was donated by Jay Ferris. The rectory on the right was added about 1900.

Methodist Rev. J. Lewis Hartsock is shown in his office around 1880. Clergymen of the period often lived very comfortably, and Reverend Hartsock's quarters appear to be well appointed. Presbyterian pastor Rev. G. F. Wile, who served the Highland church from 1866 to 1876, lived in an elegant mansion called the Pines, shown on page 68.

In 1812, the New York State legislature passed an education act that required that each town create school districts. The first schoolhouse in Highland was on Grand Street opposite Thorn's Lane. No pictures of that building exist, but here is the schoolhouse that replaced it on the same site, which opened on September 1, 1875, with 150 pupils. It was demolished in 1971.

There were 11 school districts in the town of Lloyd, and each one was required to erect a schoolhouse and to levy taxes to pay for it. School districts consolidated over the years and offered more services, but the method of taxation has not changed since 1812. This brick school building was erected near the present Highland Middle School in 1903. The wing on the left side was added around 1912, and the one on the right side was added around 1924. (Courtesy of Gail Russell.)

The Highland High School class of 1911, shown above, consisted of four young ladies. From left to right are Ethel Decker, Mabel Clearwater, Laura Palmer, and Myra Covert. In 1939, the new high school shown in the postcard below opened behind the original 1903 building, which continued to be used for elementary pupils. After a junior-senior high school was erected in 1962 on Pancake Hollow Road, the building below became an elementary school. Today it is a middle school.

1939 Bldg.

HIGHLAND HIGH SCHOOL, HIGHLAND, N. Y.   141-A

The Highland High School "Chevies" basketball team was the Ulster County Amateur and Pro champions for 1931–1932. Seen here are, from left to right, (first row) John "Sal" Marone, Phil Pampinella, ? Murphy, Kenneth Craig, and ? Upright; (second row) Vic Demare, Alan "Bonny" Hasbrouck (manager), ? Arnold, Jack McAuley, and Art Clarke (coach). Identifications were provided by Matt Murphy. (Courtesy of Matt Murphy.)

Highland's baseball team poses in front of the school around 1937. Seen here are, from left to right, (first row) Buddy Cottine, Gabe Nayles, Joe Skipp, Francis "Buddy" Rheal, Frank LaFalce, Harry Bugnali, Constancio (Cos) Trapani, and Calbert "Cal" Strongman; (second row) Elwood Sickler, Abe Deyo, Phil Oddo, John Sepolpo, Homer "Red" Muller, Dennis Murphy, Joe Trainor, Paul Sherin?, Gordon Busch, John Skipp, Charles Andola, and coach Willard Burke.

Public subscriptions were raised to pay for this monument to the 156th Regiment of New York State Volunteers, who served in the Civil War. Aaron Rhodes, himself a Civil War veteran, gave the land for it at a prominent corner leading into Highland. In the picture above is the dedication ceremony for the monument on September 19, 1908, and below it stands where it was originally placed on Milton Avenue, with Aaron Rhodes's magnificent Queen Anne–style home in the background.

Deyo's Hall is seen occupying the southwest corner of Vineyard Avenue and Main Street, now the bank corner, in this c. 1900 picture. George Washington Pratt (right) was one of the organizers of the First National Bank of Highlands in 1900, and he served as its president for 50 years. He also founded the George W. Pratt and Son lumber company in 1889.

The Highland bank originally leased space on the east side of Vineyard Avenue, but by the 1920s, it had grown to the extent that it could erect a fitting edifice of its own. Deyo's Hall, then known as the DeGraff building, was purchased, and demolition was underway in 1922.

With only the foundation of Deyo's Hall remaining on the corner, this rare view is of the original 1821 Methodist Church building, where it was situated at 4 Main Street after being moved there from the site of the present Methodist church. Also note the trolley car on Main Street.

The new limestone First National Bank building is shown above shortly after it opened in 1923. The bank building was enlarged with additions in 1952 and 1975 (below). In the 1990s, Highland's bank was purchased by the much larger M&T Bank. Due to other bank mergers, M&T wound up with three branches in Highland and decided to close this office and another office on Route 9W. The bank complex was purchased from M&T and refurbished in 1995 by Ethan P. Jackman, who opened the Highland Antique and Art Center and the Lyric Gallery in the vacant buildings. (Above, courtesy of Tim Harnett.)

The members of Highland's most exclusive ladies' society, the U.D.s, are shown in front of a Kingston hotel on the organization's 25th anniversary in 1921 (above) and at Smith's Restaurant for their 50th anniversary (below). The U.D. Society officially disbanded in 1988, and nobody ever divulged the secret of what *U.D.* stood for.

The building in the background is the original Highland Grange No. 888 hall on New Paltz Road, which was destroyed by fire in 1951 and replaced. The local Grange was organized in 1900. Other organizations often rented the use of this facility, in this case the Highland Lions Club, shown at their organizational meeting in 1930. Holding the flag in the center is Highland Ice Company owner Lorin Schantz. (Courtesy of Lindy Palladino.)

Round up Time in Highland was a highly successful annual rodeo event put on by the Lions Club in the 1950s. A "sheriff" and his "deputies" would scan the town for anyone not wearing some western garb during Round up Weekend. Such offenders would be placed in a stockade wagon and driven around the village until bailed out. (Courtesy of the Southern Ulster County Chamber of Commerce.)

Longtime Lloyd town historian Beatrice Wadlin, who wrote the book *Times and Tales of Town of Lloyd*, which was published in 1974, is shown here demonstrating spinning flax to Gail Gruner at an antique show in the town hall arranged by the Lloyd Historical Society in 1969. The spinning wheel originally belonged to Mrs. Lake, who lived in the building shown at the top of page 64.

This 1817 homestead on Main Street was built by the founder of Highland, Philip Elting. It was devised to a Masonic order in 1951 by the will of Mary Elting Maynard and became the Adonai Lodge, Free and Accepted Masons. A historical marker has been placed in front of the site by the New York State Department of Education.

The landmark "Stone House" at 121 Vineyard Avenue was built in 1846 by Col. Jacob Hasbrouck out of sandstone that was quarried behind the house. In the 1950s and 1960s, this was the home of New York State assemblyman John Wadlin, and his wife, town historian Beatrice Wadlin. (Courtesy of Vivian Yess Wadlin.)

This house on the corner of Woodside Place and Vineyard Avenue was built about 1825 by Ben and Griffen Carpenter for a Quaker named Nathaniel Selleck. Around 1900, it was the residence of Highland's most successful merchant, William E. Wilcox. Later it was the home of another well-known merchant, hardware store owner John J. Ennist. It was next sold to Harold Sutton, who had a funeral parlor in Clintondale. Today it is still the Sutton Funeral Home.

This is the Ganse house at 30 Church Street in about 1905. Dr. Ganse was a prominent dentist, whose office was across the street. He willed his house to the Ganse Foundation for charitable purposes. It has housed a nursing service, and since 1930 it has been the home of the Highland Free Library, except for some years after 1948, when it was heavily damaged by fire.

This is the Elms Hotel on Main Street, shown around 1890 before it was rebuilt into a larger structure. College rowing crews for the regattas on the Hudson River stayed here every summer. Today it is an apartment house.

Looking west on Main Street around 1900, the Elms Hotel is on the right side. Church Street is in the bottom left corner, with the stone wall and entrance to the 1897 Elting house, now the Michael Torsone Memorial Funeral Home, also on the left. Note the trolley tracks and the wagon approaching in the distance. (Courtesy of Tim Harnett.)

This is a bird's-eye view of Highland in 1969, courtesy of aerial photographer Carmine R. Iadarola. The large building in the center is the Grand Union Supermarket. After this store relocated to Bridgeview Plaza on Route 9W, this building became the headquarters of Highland Hose Company No. 1, which vacated the old firehouse in the village. To the right of this building on the other side of Milton Avenue is the Victorian mansion built by Civil War veteran Aaron Rhodes, now the site of the American Legion's Veterans' Park.

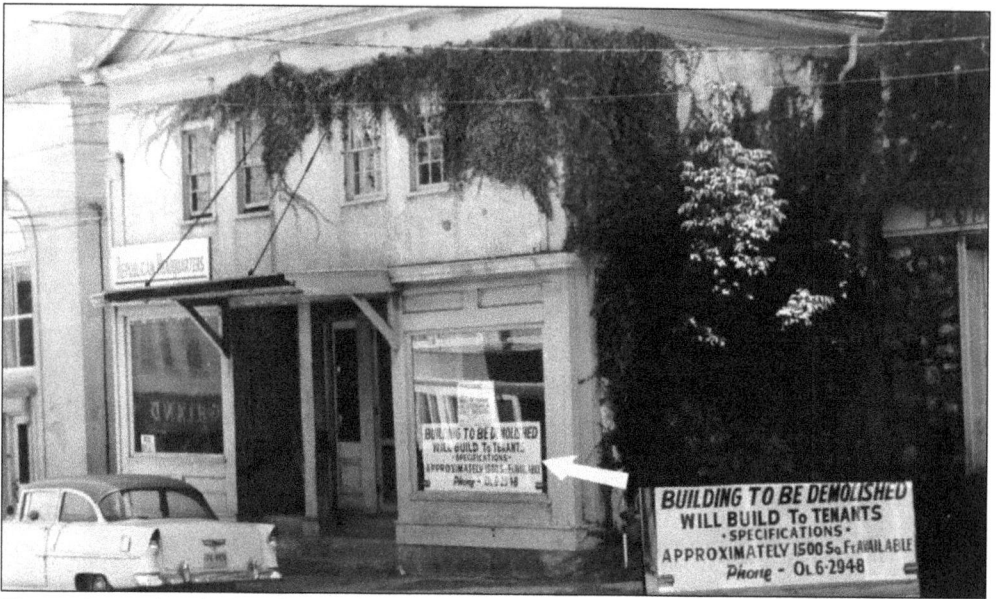

The end is at hand for the 1821 Methodist church building, seen in this 1960s photograph. Despite the offer to build a new building "to tenant's specifications," nothing else has been built on this location since the building was removed, and the area is now a private courtyard behind the bank building.

This picture shows the Highland Little League Park on Grand Street as it looked shortly after construction in the 1950s. Today the field is considerably improved, including lights that allow night games to be played. (Courtesy of the Southern Ulster County Chamber of Commerce.)

Three

RURAL LLOYD

There were many small villages in the town of Lloyd, most of which vanished without a trace as Highland became the principal community. Some of the names of these villages can still be found on the roads that led to them, such as Perkinsville Road, Riverside Road, and Oakes Road. One of the oldest villages, Centerville, at the junction of New Paltz Road, Pancake Hollow Road, and Riverside Road, is still sometimes called by that name.

In 1844, a post office named Loyd was established about a mile west of Centerville, and a community called Lloyd was in the vicinity of the Grange hall and the Loyd Rural Cemetery. Since neither Loyd nor Centerville had any formal boundaries, the names began to be used interchangeably in time.

This chapter will look at some of the buildings, farms, mills, and various establishments in the outlying parts of the town. Lloyd was considered to be somewhat of a resort area beginning in the late 19th century, with inns, boardinghouses, and hotels offering summer vacationers from one or two rooms to over 50 rooms. The more affluent moved here permanently and built elaborate Victorian mansions and great estates.

LLOYD

Scale 200 Rods to the inch

This is a map of the town of Lloyd that appeared in the 1875 F. W. Beers atlas of Ulster County. The principal villages are New Paltz Landing (which by that time was more often being called Highland Landing), Highland, Centreville, and Clintondale, which is mostly in the town of Plattekill, with only a few streets being in Lloyd. In the north central part of the town is Black Pond, now known as Chodikee Lake, which became a popular summer resort.

The Deyo-Gaffney-Schantz House shown in this c. 1880 picture was built around 1775. The gingerbread trim was added during the 19th century. It has just been purchased by the Scenic Hudson organization and will likely be restored. (Courtesy of Vivian Yess Wadlin.)

Grace Roberts's house on old Route 9W (South Roberts Road) was originally Reuben Deyo's Halfway House Inn on the Kingston Road. It was demolished in 1969 by New York State to build a new approach to the Mid-Hudson Bridge. Behind the house were large stone barns of Ulsterdorp Farms, known for its non-pasteurized milk. The barns were also demolished.

At the crossroads of the present North Road and Grand Street was a village that predates Highland. Named Nippityville, the New Paltz Landing Post Office opened here in 1821, with Dr. Barnabas Benton as the first postmaster. The above picture shows Reuben Lake's Inn on the northeast corner of North Road and Grand Street, which was built around 1795. John Benson's house (below) also dates from the late 1700s.

The Pang Yang people were followers of the mysterious Jemima Wilkinson, who having been laid out in a coffin for burial, startled mourners by arising from the casket and stating that her purpose was to organize a new religion. Originally from Connecticut, the Pang Yangers were passing through town around 1800, when they found that they could acquire land here as squatters. They built primitive shacks on some inhospitable land and earned a meager living from farming. Above is the Booth house, built around 1800, also known as the Abram Tompkins house. The picture below shows another early dwelling, the Bennett house on Chodikee Lake Road. Later this was the homestead of the Indelicato family, and part of it is still standing.

The Ezekiel Elting house on Tillson Avenue was built about 1845. It was later the residence of Clarence Elting (born 1860) and still later contractor Eugene Ossie, who built many substantial edifices in the 20th century, including the original Highland High School on Main Street, now the middle school.

This is Vineyard Avenue, looking north from Tillson Avenue, around 1910. Originally this street was part of the Modena Turnpike. In the 19th century, it was called Willow Way, after large weeping willow trees that once lined it, and finally Vineyard Avenue after fruit cultivation took hold. The first house seen was called Stonycroft.

Lakeledge, the home of Oliver J. Tillson, is opposite the end of Tillson Avenue. A house on this site dated from the 1700s, but it was destroyed by fire. When Lakeledge was erected in 1874, this Second Empire Victorian house was heralded as "the gem of all Highland homesteads." In later years, the house was divided into three apartments, but in 1991, it was purchased and restored by Ethan P. Jackman. The above photograph shows the Victorian detail on the house, while the postcard below shows the view from the artificial lakes that Tillson built in front.

Lakeledge, Tillson Residence, Highland, N. Y.

The Pines on Route 9W, originally a small Hasbrouck home, was greatly expanded in the 19th century and has been home to two physicians and one minister. Notwithstanding that New York State abolished slavery in 1827, an 1829 deed to this property shows that it was sold for four milk cows and a slave girl.

This was the 19th-century home of renowned artist Lilly Martin Spencer on Bellevue Road. She lived here from 1879 until 1892. The rambling estate overlooking the Hudson River was called Rock Nest, and it gave her inspiration for her paintings.

Dr. Charles Henry Roberts earned a good living as a dentist in Poughkeepsie, but he also made a fortune from railroad investments, and he retired at an early age to a riverside estate in the town of Lloyd. He built his first mansion, above, in 1868. About 10 years later, he built the estate shown below in an 1880 engraving on the same property. His first mansion then became a hotel, the Highland View House.

Oliver J. Tillson's son, Harry C. Tillson, bought up land on the east side of Vineyard Avenue, and built his house, above, which still stands today. It was later the home of George W. Pratt. The rustic pedestrian bridge shown below went from the roadside over the Twaalfskill Creek to this house. (Below, courtesy of Gail Russell.)

George W. Pratt's son, Harcourt J. Pratt, went into politics and was a congressman from 1924 to 1932. In 1902, he built this Edwardian mansion next to his father's house. This building has been refurbished as the Inn at Twaalfskill Bed and Breakfast. The Tillson Avenue bridge at the intersection of Vineyard Avenue is shown below in this *c.* 1890 picture. (Above, courtesy of Gail Russell.)

This is the site on which the present Highland Hose Company No. 1 firehouse is located, at the corner of Milton Avenue and Van Wagner Road. The Van Wagner–Mackey home, shown in this early-20th-century picture, stood there until a Grand Union Supermarket was erected. After Grand Union moved to Bridgeview Plaza (the present Hannaford store), its old store was remodeled to become the firehouse.

The Kisor homestead on Kisor Road was built in the early 1800s. This c. 1890 picture was taken in front of the homestead. The people are identified (from left to right) as Earl (with tie), Mr. Kisor, Mrs. Kisor, and a farmhand named Herman.

There have been many hotels, inns, and boardinghouses in the town of Lloyd, but none matched Abram E. Hasbrouck's legendary Bellevue Villa high above the Hudson, shown here in an 1892 engraving. Located on Bellevue Road with a spectacular river view, this posh resort had different custom-printed menus on the table every day. Built in 1860, it had five floors and a capacity of over 100 guests. It was destroyed by fire in 1904.

The Chodikee Lake Hotel was another famous resort that continued to operate into the 1930s. The property then became the Raymond Riordan School for Boys, and later New York State established what was called a reform school for juvenile delinquents on the site. This use continues today as the Highland Residential Center. (Courtesy of Gail Russell.)

This is the Hillaire Hotel on Grand Street in its heyday, around 1900. It was owned by Mrs. James Mack and managed by Mr. and Mrs. H. O. Palen. It played host to Syracuse University's regatta crew for two weeks each summer and was a boardinghouse for girls attending Vassar College in Poughkeepsie.

City-weary people came to Lloyd's resorts to enjoy the tranquility of country life. These two scenes are at Chodikee Lake, a favorite 19th-century destination then known as Black Pond. It is fed by the Black Creek, immortalized in the writing of naturalist John Burroughs of West Park.

The Rock House is a natural phenomenon on Illinois Mountain. Evidence of the presence of Native Americans was found in the cave, and during the War for Independence women and children are said to have taken shelter here as British general John Vaughan sailed up the Hudson River in 1777 and pummeled the little settlement at Yelverton's Landing with cannon balls.

Here the Mady K. Hasbrouck house can be seen on Weed's Mill Pond around 1895. The pond fed Amos Weed's gristmill and sawmill, shown on page 90.

This is a photograph of Schantz's Pond on Vineyard Avenue and its "lost island." In addition to being a farmer, Lorin Schantz operated the Highland Ice Company. In the winter, he harvested ice on the pond, stored it in an icehouse, and then sold it in the summer. The tiny island was lost when Schantz excavated it to allow him to cut more ice on the pond, but remnants of it have since reappeared.

The Lewiston Lake House at the corner of Route 44/55 and Chapel Hill Road was another popular place to stay in the summertime, complete with its own private pond for rowboats.

The Hotel Ottaviano, originally called Hotel Grandee, is seen as it appeared in the 1930s. It catered to summer visitors from New York City and was also a popular spot for parties. The hotel buildings were located on Kisor Road and have been demolished. (Courtesy of Sal Timperio.)

The Hotel DiPrima on North Road also was a summer destination through the 1950s but then was turned into apartments. Its restaurant is still open for business. The three brick buildings boasted "59 bedrooms with running water or private baths." It had a swimming pool, and a television set was in the lounge. (Courtesy of Vivian Yess Wadlin.)

CENTREVILLE
LLOYD P.O.

TOWN OF LLOYD
Scale 40 Rods to the inch

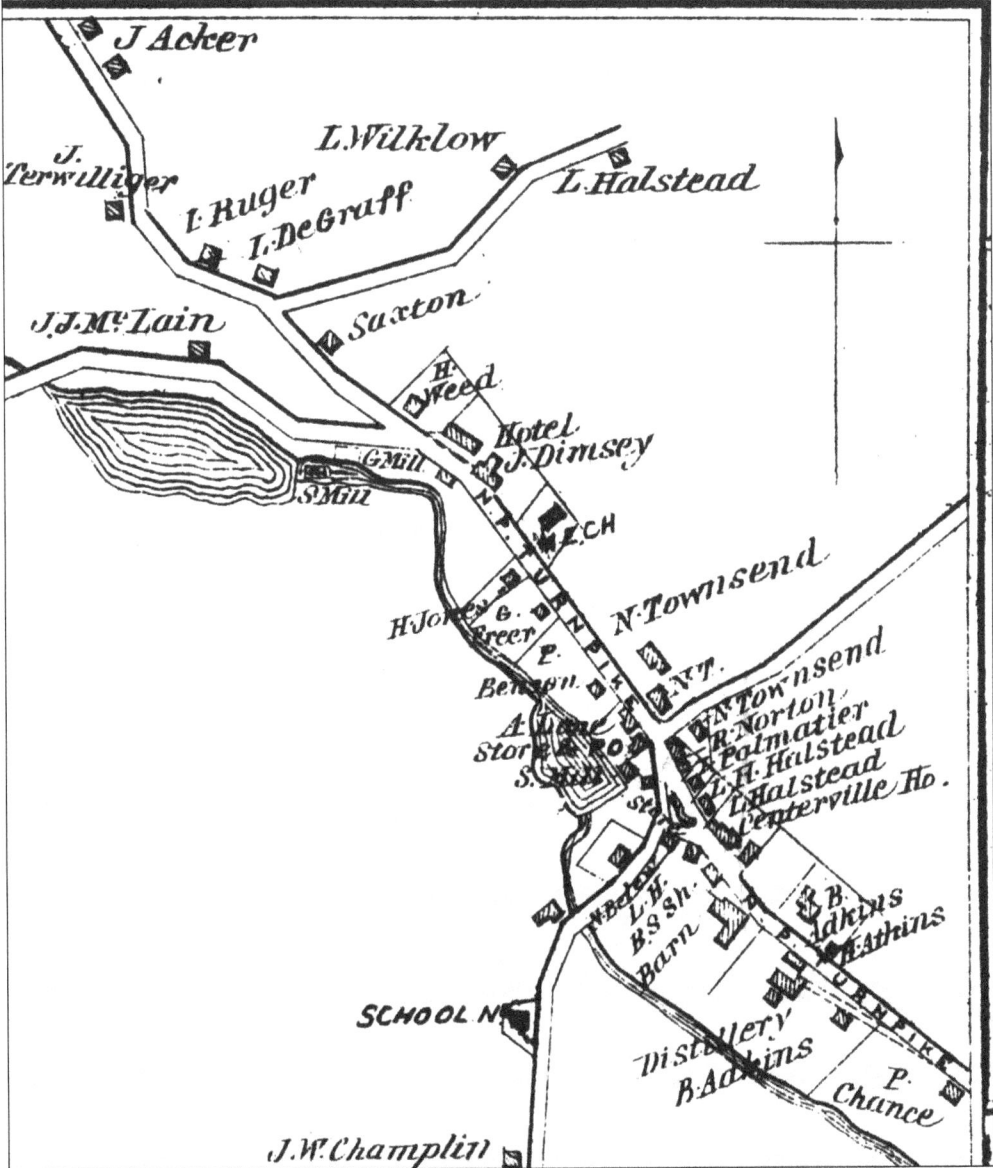

J. Acker

J. Terwilliger

L. Wilklow

I. Ruger

I. DeGraff

L. Halstead

J.J. McLain

Saxton

H. Weed

Hotel D.J. Dimsey

G. Mill

S. Mill

CH

H. Jones

G. Greer

N. Townsend

N.T.

P.

Benson

N.T.

N. Townsend

R. Norton

Polmatier

L.H. Halstead

A. Store

S. Mill

L. Halstead

Centerville Ho.

St.

W. Beton

L.H.
B.S. Sh.
Barn

B. Adkins

H. Athins

SCHOOL N

Distillery
B. Adkins

P.
Chance

J.W. Champlin

Centreville, the most notable village in rural Lloyd, is shown in this section from the 1875 F. W. Beers atlas. Some say that it was so named because it was in the center of Lloyd, but in 1829, Centreville was already on the map when Lloyd was still part of New Paltz Township. In the 20th century, the name began to be spelled *Centerville*.

Now names really get confused, because Loyd was originally another village with its own post office about a mile west of Centerville. But this *c.* 1900 postcard of "Main Street, Loyd" actually shows the intersection of Pancake Hollow Road and New Paltz Road in Centerville.

The Loyd Methodist Episcopal church was erected in 1852, west on New Paltz Road from the intersection at Centerville. In 1913, the church building had to be moved about 500 feet down the road because the Central New England Railway rerouted its tracks to go straight through the original site. The railroad paid all of the costs of moving the building. (Courtesy of Vivian Yess Wadlin.)

Kilcawley's Store at Centerville is shown in a c. 1900 postcard above, and the interior of the store, around 1890, is shown below. This store was later operated by B. C. Churchill and by Francis Madlener in the 1950s. The building was demolished in 1975. When James J. Kilcawley was appointed as postmaster of the Loyd Post Office in 1894, the post office moved into this store, but it moved back to Loyd in 1905 (see page 84).

Here the Centerville School class of 1932 is posing outside of the schoolhouse. A one-room building at that time, this structure has been enlarged and is now a private residence, south of the Centerville intersection on Pancake Hollow Road. The pupils are, from left to right, (first row) Bertha Bragg, Charles Scott, Raymond Scott, and Marie Valenti; (second row) Charles Anzalone, William Litts, and Joseph Bilyou; (third row) Louis Ciaccio, Gloria Pampinella, Mary Vasta, and Bertha Litts; (fourth row) Catherine Litts, Helen Scott, Gladys VanVliet, and Paul Vasta; (fifth row) Vera Palmateer, Rosalie Rizzo, Kay Lyons, George Realmuto, and Benjamin Bragg; (sixth row) Edward Palmateer, Michael Anzelone, and James Davis; the teacher in the doorway is Mrs. Dowd. Benjamin Bragg identified everyone in this picture from memory. (Courtesy of Benjamin Bragg Sr.)

Centerville hotel keeper John O. Litts Sr. is shown above around 1905 in front of what is now the Belvedere apartment house. This building was constructed by Lyman Halstead around 1840 and was called the Centreville Hotel. When Lloyd seceded from New Paltz in 1845, the town's organizational meeting was held in a part of this building that is no longer standing. Around the beginning of the 20th century, Litts also operated the Lloyd Hotel (below) further west on New Paltz Road. (Courtesy of Benjamin Bragg Sr.)

LLoyd John Litts Hotel

Sutton's Store, shown above around 1910, housed the Loyd Post Office from 1905 until 1933, when the post office was closed and its mail was handled by the Highland Post Office. This building is still standing on New Paltz Road, just east of the Hess gas station. "Loyd Post Office" is painted on one of the windows, and Carrie Sutton was the Loyd postmaster.

Joseph Zannucci's store at the corner of New Paltz Road and Elting's Corners Road was known as the hardware store that had every possible widget that anyone might ever need, and it also sold groceries and gasoline. The store opened in 1936 and operated until 1973. When this picture was taken, the store had already been closed for a few years, but in earlier times this corner was bustling with activity.

Berries were a profitable crop in Lloyd. A large number of strawberries were harvested on Aaron Rhodes's farm (above). The boy in front looking forward is Louis Smith Sr. Many small family farms also made a living from fruit crops. Below Elizabeth Bonin (later Mrs. Daniel Alfonso) is shown picking raspberries with her mother, Anna Bonin, on her family's Perkinsville Road farm around 1935. (Below, courtesy of Elizabeth Alfonso.)

After being harvested, fruit had to be stored until it could be shipped or sold. Once refrigeration was invented, cold storage freezers replaced root cellars. The picture above shows the c. 1920 L. G. Haviland and Sons freezer on Route 44/55, presently owned by George Sidgwick. This early freezer was quite small, and later ones such as the Michael Nardone Cold Storage freezer on North Road (below) were much larger. (Above, courtesy of George Sidgwick; below, courtesy of the Southern Ulster County Chamber of Commerce.)

One of the largest freezers in the town of Lloyd was operated by the Clintondale Cold Storage Company on Station Road. The picture above shows the building, which was mostly destroyed by fire in 1984, and the picture below shows the refrigeration machinery inside.

The Bolognesi Brothers' Hudson Valley Wine Company at Blue Point produced fine wines from local grapes between 1900 and the 1970s. Over a dozen different wines and champagnes were being produced. After Bolognesi, a new owner renamed the historic winery the Regent Champagne Cellars, but it later ceased operation. (Courtesy of Vivian Yess Wadlin.)

Schühle's Pure Grape Juice Company (pronounced Sheeley's) on Vineyard Avenue started small but became a very large operation that was later sold to a national chain. Here a processing tank headed for installation in the Schühle factory is being transported up through the village about 1910 from Highland Landing, where it had arrived by boat.

Here is the Schühle grape juice factory and how it grew. The picture above shows the original Schühle factory, which was built in 1907. In the picture below is a new addition that was built in 1911. Another addition two years later tripled the size of the plant. More additions would be put on in later years as the company continued to grow.

This was Weed's Mill, one of the last of the water-powered gristmills that once were found on every stream that had a sufficient flow of water. In the picture above is the front of the mill facing New Paltz Road (note the trolley track in front). The bottom picture shows the millpond and the rear of the mill. Thomas Halstead built the first mill on this site in 1790. In the 1840s, Silas Saxton operated the mill, and he sold it to Hiram Weed in 1856. Weed's Mill continued to be operated by the Weed family until about 1920. (Courtesy of Estelle and Thurlow Weed Jr.)

This picture shows Thomas Halstead's stone house near Weed's Mill, which is believed to have been built before 1810. His first house and barns had been made out of logs, which gave the Centerville area its early name of Log Town. (Courtesy of Estelle and Thurlow Weed Jr.)

When the Central New England Railway rerouted its track near Weed's Mill in 1914, it spelled the end of the mill. This picture shows a culvert formed out of concrete to carry track over the new line. The railroad is gone now, but the roadbed and culvert may still be seen from New Paltz Road. The mill ceased operation because waterpower became inadequate to operate it. (Courtesy of Estelle and Thurlow Weed Jr.)

This is an aerial view of the lumberyard at 128–138 Vineyard Avenue (the street at the top of the picture) that was operated for over 100 years by the firm of George W. Pratt and Son. Pratt started his first fruit crate factory and lumber business in 1874 at what came to be called Pratt's Mills, about a mile west of Highland on New Paltz Road (see page 120). Anticipating the completion of the Poughkeepsie–Highland Railroad Bridge, Pratt bought the property adjacent

to the railroad line at Vineyard Avenue and opened his new business there in 1889, the same year that trains starting running. The buildings in the foreground were crate factories, which burned down about 1969. The other buildings, including the original sawmill that spans the Twaalfskill Creek, were restored by Ethan P. Jackman in 2002.

This dam and waterfall off of Bellevue Road once powered Schantz's mill, which no longer stands. Note the large pipe on the right that diverted water to turn the waterwheel.

The Relyea Crate Factory on New Paltz Road was one of several in the town that supplied the fruit industry with crates for packing their product.

Four

THE RIVERFRONT

The riverfront was not only the site of Lloyd's first settlement and first commercial district, but it remained the town's transportation center for almost 200 years. From Yelverton's first ferry to steamboats, trains, and trolleys, all types of freight and passenger traffic moved through the landing on the Hudson.

A trail was blazed inland from the landing in 1766. It was called Squire Yelverton's Lane and followed the present course of Maple Avenue. In 1832, the New Paltz Turnpike Company completed a private toll road, also going along Maple Avenue, and then out to New Paltz village on what is now New Paltz Road. By 1875, the present River Road had been built as the New Turnpike, and what is now Maple Avenue became the Old Turnpike.

By the 1870s, Highland's riverfront landing had been built up with large wooden warehouses. On the westerly side of the street across from the warehouses, several merchants conducted stores. To the north of where the Twaalfskill Creek enters the Hudson River, the Knickerbocker Ice Company had five large icehouses. Further south along the shore, Hasbrouck and Deyo, later R. Hasbrouck Company, had a large lumberyard and coal yard and a pier for ferries and steamboats. There were also some factories in the area, notably William Davis's Highland Foundry, where a patented plow was manufactured.

In the 1880s, the West Shore Railway was constructed, with a passenger station at Highland Landing that still stands in 2009 and is now an apartment building. The railroad took a 100-foot-wide right-of-way that eliminated all of the buildings on the west side of the street across from the present Highland Landing Park. In 1882, a fire destroyed the Knickerbocker properties and several adjacent buildings. Another fire in 1888 destroyed the steamboat landing and warehouses. Some businesses rebuilt at the landing but others relocated up the hill to the thriving village of Highland.

The Poughkeepsie–Highland Railroad Bridge was completed in 1888. Although the Highland station for the bridge route was farther inland, tourists did come to Highland Landing to view the engineering feat that was considered to be one of the wonders of the world.

This dwelling was built in 1754 by Anthony Yelverton. As shown in this c. 1950 photograph, asphalt siding covered the building during much of the 20th century, and the arches under the porch are a remnant from a Victorian-style remodeling in the 19th century. The building was acquired by Ethan P. Jackman in 1999, and it has been restored to what is believed to be its original appearance.

New Paltz Landing, as the settlement at the riverfront was called during much of the 19th century, is shown on this page from the 1875 F. W. Beers atlas. The riverfront is seen to be lined with wharves and warehouses, and north of the Twaalfskill Creek are the Knickerbocker Ice Company's icehouses. There were several businesses on the turnpike, including William Davis's Highland Foundry.

Valentine Baker opened this inn at what was then called Yelverton's Landing in 1785. Later the settlement was called Baker's Landing for a while before the name New Paltz Landing came into use. Later that name gave way to the present name of Highland Landing, which will soon take on a new life as a town of Lloyd park with Hudson River access.

In addition to being a means of transportation, the Hudson River supplied an abundant amount of fish. These fishermen's huts on the river shore in 1903 were typical of many in the Lloyd area.

Elting's Hotel at Highland Landing is shown above around 1880. In later years, the additions shown below were constructed, and at different periods, it was called the Cashdollar Hotel, Simpson's Hotel, and the Mid-Hudson Hotel. It still stands and is now an apartment building.

Credited as being an engineering marvel of its time, the Poughkeepsie–Highland Railroad Bridge was finished in 1888. This picture shows a section of steel ready to be joined as the structure nears completion. Although a few trains crossed earlier, the first scheduled train crossed the span on January 1, 1899.

This c. 1890 picture shows the completed bridge from the Highland side, looking toward Poughkeepsie. The main cargo to be transported on the bridge was coal from Pennsylvania, heading east to New England. Although the bridge's promoters in Poughkeepsie said that their city would reap tremendous economic rewards from the new bridge, most trains just passed through.

A "Dinky" steam locomotive is seen here pulling a Highland trolley car across the railroad bridge around 1900. This arrangement only lasted a few years, after which all trolley passengers would have to take the ferry from Highland Landing to Poughkeepsie.

Here is an overview of the warehouses and ferry terminal at Highland Landing around 1900, with the railroad bridge in the background. Also visible is the West Shore Railroad line and a trolley car in the lower right. Highland citizens now had many choices available if they needed to travel.

The Knickerbocker icehouses at Highland Landing are shown with ice-harvesting operations in progress. The horses on treadmills would drive conveyors that brought the ice up to the top of the icehouses. These buildings later burned down, and the ice business would soon be doomed by the invention of mechanical refrigeration.

This winter of 1918 photograph shows a car driving across the frozen Hudson River. The ice was often thick enough to allow people to safely cross on foot and to cross in horse-drawn sleds. (Courtesy of Lindy Palladino.)

The West Shore Railroad passenger station at Highland is seen above in a c. 1910 picture. This building is still standing and is now an apartment house. At left, horse-drawn wagons with crates full of the produce of Lloyd farms have arrived near the station, and the crates are being loaded onto freight cars. (Courtesy of Vivian Yess Wadlin.)

The c. 1900 postcard above shows passengers from the West Shore Railroad waiting for the ferry to Poughkeepsie. Below is a picture of the ferry slip in Highland.

One of the early steam-powered ferryboats, the *C. J. Doughty* (above) ran between Highland and Poughkeepsie from 1866 to 1899. Below, the ferryboats *Brinckerhoff* and *Poughkeepsie* pass each other on a winter day in the mid-1930s. Note the Mid-Hudson Bridge in the background. Because bridge tolls were so high, the ferry service continued to operate until 1941.

The Hudson River provided the setting for intercollegiate regattas that were staged from 1898 to 1951. The above picture shows the race of 1909. Several of the regatta teams had their own boathouses. The one shown below was used by the Wisconsin crew.

In the 19th century, the steamboat *Mary Powell* reigned as the white "Queen of the Hudson." It was a daily sight in Highland, but stopped at Poughkeepsie, where the Highland ferry would meet the steamboat. Its run between Kingston and Manhattan took about five hours each way, but entertainment was provided onboard by the Mary Powell Orchestra.

The Mid-Hudson Bridge was opened in 1930, but the tolls were so high that people who were not in a hurry could save money by taking the ferry across the river instead of the bridge. The ferry kept operating until 1941. Here the Hudson River Day Line's *Peter Stuyvesant* passes under the Mid-Hudson Bridge around 1950.

Five

INLAND TRANSPORTATION

In the days before automobiles, the unpaved streets of the town were full of ruts made by the thin wheels of wagons. As primitive as that may seem today, the people riding in their horse-drawn buggies were often seen in fine attire that attests to the fact that despite the hardships of life before the age of invention, the citizens had a high sense of self-respect and dignity.

The West Shore Railroad along the Hudson River opened in 1883, and the first scheduled passenger train over the Poughkeepsie–Highland Railroad Bridge ran on January 1, 1899. On the Highland side of the bridge, the Hudson Connecting Railroad Company had laid tracks to Campbell Hall and offered one train a day to and from Poughkeepsie. That line was short-lived, because the Central New England Railway bought it and many other small lines to build the Poughkeepsie Bridge Route through New York and Connecticut. Shipping by railroad proved to be more economical than by riverboat, and river traffic began to decline.

The final link in Highland's transportation system was an electric railway or trolley line that ran from the rail and ferry terminals at the riverfront all the way to the village of New Paltz. Acquiring a right-of-way for the trolley was easy. The newly formed trolley company bought the private New Paltz Turnpike toll road in 1894 and proceeded to lay tracks along the old turnpike road. The first scheduled trolley ran on August 12, 1897, but the builders could not foresee the success of automobiles. The trolley made its last run in 1925.

This is what Vineyard Avenue in front of Pratt's Lumber Yard looked like around 1890, when a carriage provided the best way to get to the village of Highland. On the left is part of the Twaalfskill Creek, which was called Willow Brook after the large willow trees. As was the case with all other streets and roads at that time, the road is unpaved and full of ruts.

Here a buggy stops for supplies at Schoonmaker and VanEtten's dry goods store around 1880. Customers had plenty of choices once they got to Highland. They could ride around town to shop at W. E. Wilcox's store or Byron Clearwater's, and see who had the best merchandise and prices.

Dr. George S. LaMoree (in wagon) is ready to leave his barn and make a house call around 1890. This well-respected physician served several terms on the Highland Board of Education and was involved in building the new brick school in 1903. He was also the Highland postmaster from 1916 to 1922. The man holding the horse is Charles Freer.

This highway crew of 1900 had no machinery, just laborers with picks and shovels.

Cars are not needed to have traffic accidents. This sled full of hay seems to have hit a bump in the road near 6 Main Street in Highland. On the left is George E. Clinton's market, which sold produce, fish, and confections. At the end of the street in the upper right is the tower of the Ganse residence, which has housed the Highland Free Library for over 75 years.

In the winter, a sled was still a good way to get to the village around 1935, when this party was setting out from Perkinsville Road and heading to Highland. From left to right are an unidentified farmhand (holding cat), Mr. Preiss, Mrs. Preiss, daughter Ruth Preiss, Elizabeth Bonin (later Mrs. Daniel Alfonso), and her mother, Anna Bonin. (Courtesy of Elizabeth Alfonso.)

The c. 1895 picture above shows a freight train roaring down the north–south West Shore Railroad through Lloyd between Albany, New York, and Weehawken, New Jersey. In 1936, the West Shore Railroad ran the special train below to bring college crews to the regatta at Highland. But the growing popularity and convenience of the automobile were making passenger traffic less profitable for the railroads, and a ride on the West Shore line would soon be a thing of the past. (Below, courtesy of Vivian Yess Wadlin.)

This scene in 1889 shows the Highland stop on the Poughkeepsie–Highland Railroad Bridge route. It was located off of Vineyard Avenue, just west of the new George W. Pratt and Son lumberyard. The station house had not yet been erected.

Later on, the Central New England Railway built this passenger station at Highland. Franklin D. Roosevelt often took this line to Highland and then was driven from this station across the Mid-Hudson Bridge to his home in Hyde Park. The station was demolished around 1973. (Courtesy of Edmund R. Hopper.)

In this picture, a railroad crew is seen clearing ice from the Central New England Railway tracks near New Paltz Road in the 1930s. The Central New England Railway brought passengers and freight to Highland over the colossal Poughkeepsie–Highland Railroad Bridge. The line was part of the New York, New Haven and Hartford Railroad when this picture was taken.

Railroading was not without its hazards, and several accidents occurred over the years. Here a train wreck on the Central New England Railway near the Loyd station is being cleared from the tracks on November 15, 1919. Note the second set of tracks in the foreground, which was for the trolley. Loyd was a transfer point between the railway and the trolley. This scene was across the road just east of the present Highland Hose Company No. 2 firehouse.

This tollhouse stood on the New Paltz Turnpike near the present junction of River Road and Maple Avenue at White Street. A private company built the turnpike between 1820 and 1832, and the toll for a one-horse wagon was 3¢. When this picture was taken sometime after 1897, the trolley tracks were in place and tolls were no longer being collected from wagons.

Highland's largest transportation venture was a trolley car line from the ferry and railway terminals at Highland Landing to the Wallkill Valley Railroad line in New Paltz village. This scene shows trolley tracks being laid in the center of town during the summer of 1897.

The town is decked out to celebrate Glad Day on August 24, 1915. The event marked the opening of a brick-paved state road from Highland Landing to the village of Highland. This was the largest celebration that Highland has ever seen, with newspaper accounts placing the crowd at about 5,000. The celebration covered the front page of the *Poughkeepsie Star* as well as the local *Highland Post*. The project cost $130,000 (equivalent to $2.715 million with inflation to 2009 dollars). In these two pictures, spectators are waiting for the parade to start on Main Street (above) and Vineyard Avenue (below). (Below, courtesy of Gail Russell.)

The Glad Day parade included the Highland Citizens' Band, which was led by drum major B. Gedney (above), and John Schühle's grape juice wagon with local Camp Fire Girls aboard (below). The committee that organized Glad Day was headed by storekeeper William E. Wilcox, and another storekeeper, Byron Clearwater, was parade marshal. The parade was led by the band and started out from the village square toward the river. Following them came four children riding ponies, then the Boy Scouts, and then a "long line of plain, every-day citizens." Following that were automobiles, "upwards of eighty by actual count," and all decorated for the occasion. Then came floats sponsored by local and Poughkeepsie businesses.

Here is the reason that everyone was glad. The picture above shows River Road before the state upgraded it, and the picture below shows the same stretch of roadway afterward. After the parade reached the railroad at Highland Landing, it returned to the village, went down Vineyard Avenue to Oliver J. Tillson's Lakeledge estate, and then came back to the village where the procession ended around noon. Most people took lunch at restaurants and from various vendors, including the local women's suffrage committee, which served over 150 meals that day, and from a lunch counter on the Methodist church grounds. Around 2:00 p.m., ceremonies began with a band concert in the churchyard.

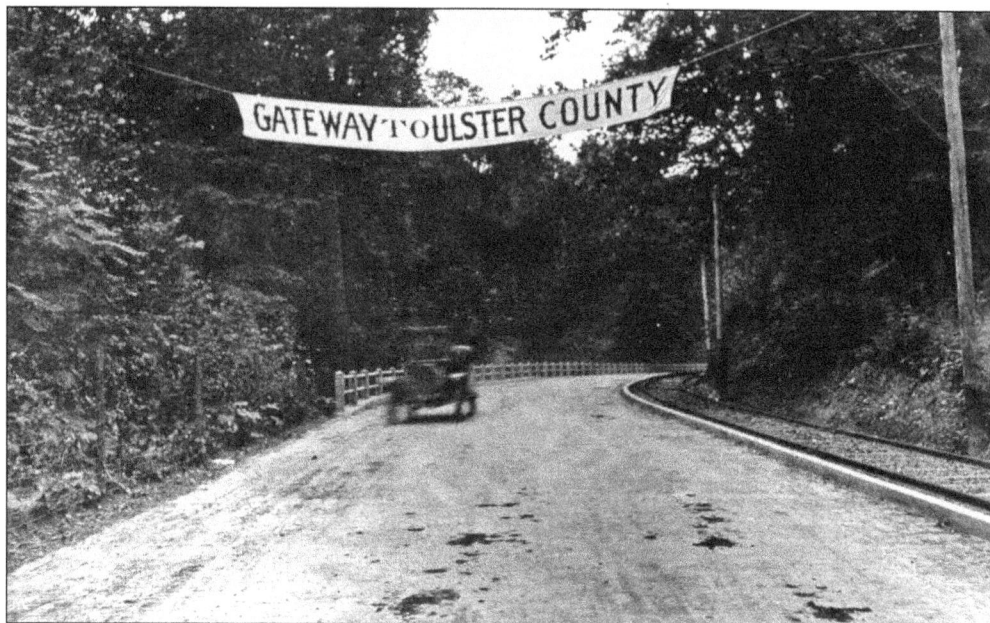

This "Gateway to Ulster County" banner remained on River Road after Glad Day to welcome visitors arriving in Highland by rail and ferryboat. Highland really was a gateway, and the village had found a new identity as a local transportation hub. Business boomed in downtown Highland—hotels, restaurants, automobile shops, and gasoline dealers all catered to the traveling public. Highland merchants sold everything that one might need for the home and for the farm.

This wagon is being driven by a very prominent citizen of the day, John Schühle of Schühle's Pure Grape Juice Company, with his favorite horse, Nell. The Twaalfskill Creek flows alongside River Road, which makes the route very scenic and also provided the force for several water-powered mills. However, the road is subject to flooding from the stream, which periodically causes major damage.

Here River Road passes the early-19th-century home that belonged to Lloyd town supervisor Philip Schantz, who served for 19 years at various times between 1893 and 1928. Located opposite Bellevue Road, Schantz operated the mill across the street. His brother, Lorin Schantz, operated another mill on Vineyard Avenue, also powered by the Twaalfskill.

Here is a scene that was once made into a postcard titled "The Parting of the Ways." It shows the new highway and trolley line on the left (now River Road), and the old turnpike on the right (now Maple Avenue). Note the trolley poles on the left above the tracks. The house on the right dates from about 1850 and now has a 20th-century saltbox addition on the rear.

This was George W. Pratt's first lumberyard and crate factory at Pratt's Mills, just west of Highland on New Paltz Road, which opened in 1874. The Central New England Railway tracks (with steam engine) are in the background, and trolley tracks are in the foreground. Pratt's Mills was the only place where trolley cars could be transferred onto the railway line to be pulled across the Poughkeepsie–Highland Railroad Bridge by a locomotive.

Here a locomotive nicknamed the "Dinky" is ready to pull a small railway coach and a trolley car over the bridge to Poughkeepsie. The locomotive was actually a switching engine used in the Poughkeepsie railroad yards. The Dinky train ran between Pratt's Mills and the Poughkeepsie station on Parker Avenue, stopping at the Highland station off of Vineyard Avenue. This was a summer service and was discontinued in 1902.

Lloyd Power House

This powerhouse at Loyd generated electricity to run the trolley line. Coal-fired steam engines ran direct current generators that produced power, which was transmitted to the trolley cable that ran above the tracks. After the trolley stopped running, the building was a machine shop and later a snack food distributor's warehouse. In 1979, voters in the Highland Fire District approved purchasing the building, and it is now the Highland Hose Company No. 2 firehouse.

This picture shows one of the generators inside the trolley powerhouse at Loyd. It turned out that if two trolley cars on the line were trying to go up hills at the same time, the amount of power produced was not sufficient. One car might have to wait for the other to get over the hill before proceeding.

This tiny trolley car ran on its own line a distance of only 500 feet between the end of the main trolley line at Highland Landing and the ferry slip. Passengers had to transfer their baggage from one car to the other, because the trolleys could not cross the railroad tracks. Since this car had only one truck (set of wheels), the short ride could be anything but smooth.

122

This picture shows trolley car No. 9, named *Loyd*. Trolleys ran every half-hour from Highland village and hourly from New Paltz village to the river, where they would meet the ferry to Poughkeepsie. Passengers could flag down a trolley car or leave one anywhere along its route, although timetables showed official stops in Highland, Pratt's Mills, Centerville, Lloyd, Elting's Corners, Ohioville, and Putt Corners.

This picture shows trolley car No. 14. The motorman and conductor seem to be enjoying the attention of the photographer, without too much regard for the passengers who are seen seated inside the car. This was the only trolley line in Ulster County that went from one village to another, a distance of about nine miles. At the New Paltz end, stagecoaches would meet the trolley to take passengers to mountain resorts. (Courtesy of Vivian Yess Wadlin.)

Trolley car No. 4 and an open car are seen at Brooks Crossing, going over the Central New England Railway tracks. This roller coaster–type arrangement was necessary because the railway, fearing possible collisions, would not let the trolley cross its tracks on the same level. The open car was used for summer excursions. The trolley line also operated a self-propelled freight car.

This is Lorensen's Square Deal Garage in 1928. It was primarily a repair shop but also sold Goodrich tires, batteries, oil, and of course gasoline, with pumps right at the curb. Later this building was the home of the Berean Press, operated by Harold C. Berean Sr. and later by his son. Berean started out as a job printer, but he later expanded into the newspaper business and published the *Highland News* from 1937 to 1972.

Here are two views of Smith's Garage at 79 Vineyard Avenue, with the latest car models on display. The picture above was taken around 1915, when Smith was a Ford dealer, and the lower one about 25 years later, when he had a Chevrolet and Buick dealership. The dealership later relocated to Route 9W, and the building then housed the Highland Post Office. When the First National Bank needed space for a data-processing center, it bought the building and connected it to the main part of the bank with a passageway. During the 1990s, the Lyric Gallery, under the direction of Naomi Jackman, used this building to put on art exhibits and classical concerts that brought the area's leading artists and musicians to Highland.

This is a c. 1950 aerial view of the Bridge Circle, a traffic circle that was used to access the Mid-Hudson Bridge. Route 9W is shown running left to right. Traffic would turn off of Route 9W and head up Haviland Road to get onto the bridge. In the upper center is the Poughkeepsie–Highland Railroad Bridge crossing the Hudson River. Haviland Road goes to the right and the Mid-Hudson Bridge is not visible in this view. (Courtesy of the Southern Ulster County Chamber of Commerce.)

George's Rest was a 1950s version of a fast-food restaurant on the Bridge Circle. Serving a whole fried chicken for $1, or half of one for 50¢, the restaurant featured home-cooked dinners, waffles, and homemade pies. George's Rest also made its own ice cream and had Mobil gasoline pumps. A Sunoco gas station and convenience store are now on this site.

On October 30, 1943, this freight train derailed near Pratt's Mills on the former Central New England Railway line, which was then owned by the New York, New Haven and Hartford Railroad. Twenty-seven tank cars carrying high-octane airplane gasoline that was intended for use in World War II burst into flames, but firemen were able to save the other cars. Two cars were carrying dynamite, but they were at the rear of the train and the dynamite did not explode. Three houses and some outbuildings were also destroyed, but nobody was seriously injured. Total damages were estimated to be about $600,000. The derailment was caused by two young boys who had put stones on the track "to see what would happen."

Visit us at
arcadiapublishing.com